PUBLIC LIBRARY, DISTRICT OF COLUMBIA

W9-CIK-450

The *Untold Story*
of the
Black
Regiment

Fighting in the
Revolutionary War

by Michael Burgan

Content Adviser: Alan Gilbert, PhD
John Evans Professor
University of Denver

COMPASS POINT BOOKS
a capstone imprint

Compass Point Books are published by Capstone,
1710 Roe Crest Drive, North Mankato, Minnesota 56003
www.capstonepub.com

Copyright © 2015 by Compass Point Books, a Capstone imprint.
All rights reserved. No part of this publication may be reproduced in whole
or in part, or stored in a retrieval system, or transmitted in any form or by any
means, electronic, mechanical, photocopying, recording, or otherwise, without
written permission of the publisher.

Editorial Credits
Jennifer Huston, editor; Heidi Thompson, designer;
Eric Gohl, media researcher; Laura Manthe, production specialist;
Kathleen Baxter, library consultant

Photo Credits
Alamy: North Wind Picture Archives, 11, 41, 51, Stan Tess, 31; Courtesy of
Army Art Collection, U.S. Army Center of Military History: 5, 14; Courtesy of
Bobb Vann, artist: 25; Corbis: Bettmann, 7; Courtesy of David R. Wagner, artist:
cover, 29; Getty Images: DeAgostini, 35, Ed Vebell, 17, Hulton Archive, 8,
MPI, 12; Glow Images: SuperStock, 46; The Granger Collection, NYC: 48;
The Image Works: akg-images/Sotheby's, 56–57; Library of Congress: 21, 43;
Portrait, James Forten, Leon Gardiner Collection of American Negro
Historical Records and HSP Treasures Collection, The Historical Society
of Pennsylvania: 53; SuperStock: 26; Wikimedia: Public Domain, 23, 33;
www.historicalimagebank.com, Painting by Don Troiani: 38

Design Elements: Shutterstock

Library of Congress Cataloging-in-Publication Data
Burgan, Michael.
  The Untold Story of the Black Regiment: Fighting in the Revolutionary War/
by Michael Burgan.
    pages cm. —What You Didn't Know About the American Revolution
    Includes bibliographical references and index.
    ISBN 978-0-7565-4975-6 (library binding)
    ISBN 978-0-7565-4979-4 (paperback)
    ISBN 978-0-7565-4983-1 (ebook PDF)
1. United States—History—Revolution, 1775–1783—Participation, African
American—Juvenile literature. 2. African American soldiers—History—
18th century—Juvenile literature. I. Title.

E269.N3B87 2015
973.3'44—dc23   2014038069

Printed in the United States of America in Stevens Point, Wisconsin.
092014   008479WZS15

TABLE OF
Contents

CHAPTER One

The Road to War

A drumbeat broke the early morning silence in Lexington, Massachusetts, on April 19, 1775. The steady rhythm was an alarm, telling the townspeople that British soldiers were approaching. The Redcoats had come from Boston and were marching northwest on their way to nearby Concord. Members of Lexington's militia grabbed their guns and headed off to meet the advancing troops.

Among the 70 or so men who answered the drummer's call was Prince Estabrook, a black slave. With the permission of his master, Estabrook had volunteered to join the Lexington militia and was ready to fight the British if war came. No one had promised Estabrook his freedom in return for risking his life. He did it out of patriotism, although he did win his freedom by the end of the war. Estabrook also earned the distinction of

When the first shots of the Battle of Lexington rang out, approximately 70 militiamen from Massachusetts, including Prince Estabrook, participated in the battle.

becoming the first black man to fight in the Revolutionary War. When he and the other militiamen confronted the British that fateful morning, the Revolutionary War officially began.

For Estabrook and other slaves, the Revolutionary War gave them the chance to gain their freedom. Across the 13 colonies, thousands of blacks bravely served during the War of Independence.

Anger Turns to Violence

The roots of the Revolutionary War reached back more than a decade before the Battle of Lexington. After winning the French and Indian War (1754–1763), Great Britain took control of all of France's territory in Canada and its holdings east of the Mississippi River. During that war both white and black soldiers from Britain's 13 American Colonies helped battle the French. But instead of being grateful for their service, Parliament charged the Americans higher taxes to help Great Britain defend its new lands.

In 1764 a law called the Sugar Act imposed a tax on sugar and molasses in the American Colonies. Some colonists wrote articles and pamphlets and sent written protests to Parliament protesting the Sugar Act.

Americans grew even angrier the next year when Parliament passed the Stamp Act. This law introduced a new tax on paper goods and documents. Colonists in Boston felt they were being unfairly taxed without receiving proper representation in Parliament. At times the protests against the taxes and British policies turned violent, which in 1768 led England's King George III to send troops to Boston to restore order. Patriots there despised the soldiers, especially when they tried to earn extra money by taking jobs away from residents.

The anger boiled over on the night of March 5, 1770, in what came to be known as the Boston Massacre. When a few young men insulted a British soldier on guard duty, the soldier struck one of them with his gun. When the injured man cried out in pain, more residents and soldiers poured into

Two British soldiers were found guilty of manslaughter following the Boston Massacre. As punishment, their hands were branded with the letter "M."

the street. The angry American crowd swarmed to about 400 people. Leading them was a man named Crispus Attucks.

Attucks was the son of an African father and an American Indian mother. Like most blacks in the American Colonies, Attucks had once been a slave. But he had escaped from his master 20 years earlier and had lived as a free man ever since.

Attucks allegedly pushed aside the bayonet on a soldier's gun and then knocked him to the ground. All around them, Americans threw snowballs, and some swung sticks. Panicked and outnumbered, the British soldiers fired into the crowd. Attucks and four other men died from gunshot wounds.

Most slaves in Colonial America lived in the South. Many worked on large plantations picking tobacco and later cotton, as seen here.

Blacks in Colonial America

To many patriots, Attucks was a hero during the Boston Massacre because he had stood up to the British soldiers who often bullied Americans. But for most blacks across the American Colonies, "freedom" was just a word. In their daily lives, black men, women, and children worked as slaves—the property of another person. Conditions for enslaved people varied across the colonies, but slavery existed in each one. Merchants got rich by bringing slaves from Africa or the Caribbean to America.

The first African slaves had come to North America with Dutch explorers in 1619, arriving in Virginia. Although they had been captured from a slave ship, some went to work as indentured servants, who were able to earn their freedom after serving a master for a number of years.

In the 18th century, the number of slaves in the South exploded. By some accounts, in 1763 slave masters in the Carolinas, Maryland, and Virginia owned 85 percent of the slaves in the American Colonies. In 1770 in Virginia alone, there were about 200,000 slaves working in the fields harvesting tobacco and other crops.

The estimated population of blacks in the American Colonies at that time was about 500,000—which was roughly 20 percent of the entire Colonial population. Only about one in four whites owned slaves, meaning that some people owned many to operate their large plantations. Slaves were routinely subject to beatings, and many were killed to set an example to others to obey their masters. Families were often torn apart as children were taken away from their parents and sold to other masters.

Population of Colonial America at the Start of the Revolutionary War (1775)

Region	White	Black	Percentage of Total Population
New England Connecticut, Massachusetts, New Hampshire, Rhode Island, Vermont	97%	3%	26%
Mid-Atlantic New Jersey, New York, Pennsylvania	94%	6%	24%
Upper South Delaware, Maryland, Virginia	63%	37%	31%
Lower South Georgia, North Carolina, South Carolina	59%	41%	17%
West Kentucky, Tennessee	83%	17%	1%
Total Population	79%	21%	100%*
Population	1.94 million	520,000	2.46 million

*Note: 1775 figures averaged from 1770 and 1780 figures.
Percentages do not add to 100 because of rounding.
Source: Lemon, James T., *Colonial America in the Eighteenth Century*, p. 123

Slave owners who lived in cities or ran small farms usually owned only a few slaves. The slaves in cities typically worked in their masters' homes or as laborers. Their jobs might involve making bricks or working on ships. Some slaves brought skills they had learned in Africa, such as carpentry, growing rice, and working with iron.

The number of free blacks in America grew during the Colonial era, but it never reached more than about 10 percent of the African-American population. Some slaves, like Crispus Attucks, escaped from their masters and managed to avoid recapture. Some masters allowed their slaves to earn money by working for other people. These slaves saved their earnings and used it to buy their own freedom. And a small number of slave owners left wills that called for their slaves to be set free after the master's death.

Even when they gained their freedom, some blacks in the American Colonies faced legal restrictions. Some colonies did not allow them to vote or own property. And sometimes the children of free blacks were taken from their parents and were forced to work as indentured servants for up to 24 years.

For most slave owners, slavery came down to economics. It was simply cheaper to buy slaves than it was to hire workers. Some people also justified slavery with racist thinking. They thought they were better than blacks, so it was all right to treat them as property. Although a considerable number of white Americans wanted to abolish slavery, most accepted it—even as they called for their own freedom from Great Britain.

On some southern plantations, slaves harvested sugarcane. It was sweaty, backbreaking work, and the slaves often worked from sunup to sundown.

During the Boston Tea Party on December 16, 1773, colonists dump 46 tons (42 metric tons) of tea into Boston Harbor.

Reaching a Crisis

The Boston Massacre did not play a direct role in starting the Revolutionary War, but it did set a spark. And a December 1773 revolt in Boston only added fuel to the fire. At what became known as the Boston Tea Party, black and white patriots threw hundreds of crates of tea into the harbor to protest yet another tax. In response, Parliament passed a series of laws that the Americans called the Intolerable Acts. Among other things, the laws called for placing a British military governor in charge of Massachusetts, closing down Boston Harbor, and ending the rule of local governments in the colony.

Although they targeted only Massachusetts, the Intolerable Acts alarmed patriots across the 13 colonies. Patriots in the other colonies realized that the laws limited long-held freedoms in Massachusetts, and some worried that the British would clamp down on them in the same way. In 1774 local militias in Massachusetts prepared for a possible battle. That September, patriot leaders from 12 colonies (Georgia did not take part) met in Philadelphia at the Continental Congress. They discussed how all of the American Colonies could work together to preserve their freedoms.

Slaves were also thinking about their own freedom. They heard their masters and other patriots say that they did not want to be slaves to the British. The slaves in the American Colonies thought the call for freedom should apply to them as well.

Even before the Boston Tea Party, some slaves in Massachusetts had filed petitions to the governor and the Colonial legislature asking for their freedom. But Colonial lawmakers ignored these pleas, even as they continued to discuss the loss of their own rights and freedom from British rule.

A Call for Freedom

In April 1773 Peter Bestes, Sambo Freeman, Felix Holbrook, and Chester Joie submitted a petition to Massachusetts lawmakers requesting their freedom. Here is part of what they wrote:

"We expect great things from men who have made such a noble stand against the designs of their fellow-men to enslave them. We cannot but wish and hope Sir, that you will ... give us that ample relief which, as men, we have a natural right to."

CHAPTER *Two*

First Blacks on the Battlefield

On April 19, 1775, the conflict between the American Colonies and Great Britain officially became a war. The night before, British troops left Boston on their way to Concord, where they hoped

The first shots of the Battle of Concord rang out when local Minutemen encountered the British at North Bridge.

to capture weapons and patriot leaders Samuel Adams and John Hancock. Early on the morning of April 19, the British passed through the town of Lexington, where specially trained militia known as Minutemen waited for them. Prince Estabrook was among them. Captain John Parker instructed the Minutemen to hold their fire until fired upon. When British Major John Pitcairn yelled, "Lay down your arms!" the Americans looked to Parker to see what they should do. Realizing he was outnumbered, Parker told his men to leave. But suddenly without warning, shooting erupted. It is unclear who fired that first shot, but the two sides exchanged fire. The Revolutionary War had officially begun.

As smoke filled the air, the British officers ordered their men to stop firing. But as one officer later said, "The men were so wild, they could hear no orders."

Finally, a British drummer beat out the signal to stop firing. This time the soldiers obeyed. When the shooting ended, eight Americans were dead and 10 others were wounded. Only one British soldier was injured. The Redcoats set off for their original destination of Concord, and the fighting intensified as the day progressed.

As the fighting continued, more blacks answered the call to battle the British, including Peter Salem, whose master had already granted his freedom so he could fight. He fought at North Bridge, where the two sides first exchanged fire in Concord. By day's end, militia from around Concord had come to fend off the British, who were forced to retreat to Boston.

Key Battles of the First Months

After Lexington and Concord, the fighting spread farther north. On May 10 a small force led by Ethan Allen and Benedict Arnold seized Fort Ticonderoga in New York from the British. Lemuel Haynes took part in this raid in which the Americans surprised the outnumbered British at dawn. The patriots took the fort without firing a shot. They also captured numerous pieces of artillery.

Barzillai Lew was among a handful of black soldiers at Fort Ticonderoga. He had earlier served with the British during the French and Indian War. Lew was a free black man and a skilled musician who played the fife. Although he didn't have a chance to fire on the enemy during the siege of Fort Ticonderoga, Lew was one of more than a hundred blacks and American Indians known to have fought at the next major battle, Bunker Hill.

The Needs of Wartime

The first Continental Congress did not want blacks—slave or free—to serve in the militias. Its members feared that armed blacks might lead slave rebellions. But in practice most local militia groups ignored laws that prevented blacks from serving. When Prince Estabrook volunteered for the Lexington militia, the white members voted to accept him. When war came and the army needed soldiers, concerns about someone's skin color were unimportant. That fact would come into play often during the Revolutionary War.

The Redcoats overpowered the patriots at the Battle of Bunker Hill.

On June 17 the British stormed a hill defended by the patriots on the north side of Boston. Behind fences and rocks, the Americans cut down British soldiers who trudged up the hill carrying heavy backpacks. The patriots managed to hold off two waves of British attacks. During their third attack, the British finally took the hill but at a heavy loss. More than 1,000 Redcoats were killed that day, compared to 400 Americans. One of the dead was British Major John Pitcairn. By some accounts, Peter Salem had shot him in the head.

Another free black man who won praise that day was Salem Poor, who also killed a British officer. Later a group of American officers noted that Poor "behaved like an Experienced Officer, as Well as an Excellent Soldier."

Serving in Virginia

While the first major battles of the Revolutionary War were raging in the North, fighting was also taking place in the South. With promises of freedom, the British hoped to use blacks as soldiers in their quest to end the American rebellion. As early as 1772, Lord Dunmore, the royal governor of Virginia, believed that if Great Britain and the colonies ever went to war, blacks who were granted their freedom by the British would eagerly fight their former masters.

Once war broke out, Dunmore warned patriot slave owners in Virginia that he would arm their slaves if they joined the revolution. The slave owners genuinely feared a slave rebellion fueled by Dunmore. But instead of backing

By His Excellency the Right Honorable JOHN Earl of DUNMORE, His Majesty's Lieutenant and Governor General of the Colony and Dominion of Virginia, and Vice Admiral of the same.

A PROCLAMATION.

As I have ever entertained Hopes that and Accommodation might have taken Place between Great-Britain and this Colony, without being compelled by my Duty to this most disagreeable but now absolutely necessary Step, rendered so by a Body of armed Men unlawfully assembled, firing on His Majesty's Tenders, and the formation of an Army, and that Army now on their March to attack His Majesty's Troops and destroy the well disposed Subjects of this Colony. To defeat such treasonable Purposes, and that all such Traitors, and the Abettors, may be brought to Justice, and that the Peace, and good Order of this Colony may be again restored, which the ordinary Course of the Civil Law is unable to effect; I have thought fit to issue this my Proclamation, hereby declaring, that until the aforesaid good Purposes can be obtained, I do in Virtue of the Power and Authority to ME given, by his Majesty, determine to execute Martial Law, and cause the same to be executed throughout this Colony: and to the end that Peace and good Order may the sooner be restored, I do require every Person capable of bearing Arms, to resort to His Majesty's STANDARD, or be looked upon as Traitors to His Majesty's Crown and Government, and thereby become liable to the Penalty the Law inflicts upon such Offences; such as forfeiture of Life, confiscation of Lands, &c, &c. And I do hereby further declare all indentured Servants, Negroes or others, (appertaining to Rebels,) free that are able and willing to bear Arms, they joining His Majesty's Troops as soon as may be, for the more speedily reducing this Colony to a proper Sense of their Duty to His Majesty's Crown and Dignity. I do further order, and require, all His Majesty's Liege Subjects, to retain their Quitrents, or any other Taxes due or that may become due, in their own Custody, till such Time as Peace may be again restored to this at present most unhappy Country, or demanded of them for their former falutary Purposes, by Officers properly authorised to receive the same.

GIVEN under my Hand on board the Ship WILLIAM, of Norfolk, the ,th Day of November, in the Sixteenth Year of His Majesty's Reign.

DUNMORE.

(GOD save the KING.)

Lord Dunmore's Proclamation

down, many patriots, particularly in the North, began to think about freeing and recruiting slaves.

Back in London, some members of Parliament supported the idea of recruiting slaves to fight for the British. But ultimately a proposal to make this happen was defeated. Even without Parliament's approval, in November 1775 Lord Dunmore issued a proclamation. He would carry out his earlier promise to free slaves who fought for the British. However, the governor basically wanted to reduce the number of patriots he had to fight. He was less concerned about the freedom of blacks.

Even so, over the next several weeks, about 300 slaves answered his call. They were ready to fight the patriots if it guaranteed their freedom. In all, about 800 fought for Dunmore. The newly freed slaves received weapons and uniforms that included a badge with the words "Liberty to Slaves." They were known as Lord Dunmore's Ethiopian Regiment, the name referring to the African nation of Ethiopia.

Excerpt from Lord Dunmore's Proclamation

And I do hereby further declare all indentured Servants, Negroes, or others, (appertaining to Rebels,) free that are able and willing to bear Arms, they joining His Majesty's Troops as soon as may be, for the more speedily reducing this Colony to a proper Sense of their Duty, to His Majesty's Crown and Dignity.

Washington and Black Soldiers

While Dunmore recruited slaves for the British Army, George Washington was trying to decide what to do about black soldiers in his army. When Washington arrived in Boston in July 1775, he was shocked to see blacks—both slaves and free—fighting side by side for the patriots.

Washington was a slave owner, so he was uncomfortable with the sight of blacks armed with guns. But as commander of the Continental army, he also realized that he needed all the soldiers he could get. Therefore, he didn't discharge the blacks serving under him. But he did stop recruiting new black soldiers, and in November, Congress voted to keep blacks out of the Continental army altogether.

But when Washington heard about Lord Dunmore's call for blacks to escape and fight for the British, he had a change of heart. Dunmore had found a way to recruit more troops and at the same time embarrass the Americans, who talked of liberty and freedom for all but were not willing to free their slaves. At the end of 1775, despite Congress' earlier ruling, Washington told his generals they could once again recruit free blacks. He wrote to Congress that "free Negroes who have served in the Army, are

Did You Know?

After the Revolutionary War, the U.S. Army would not be integrated again until 1948.

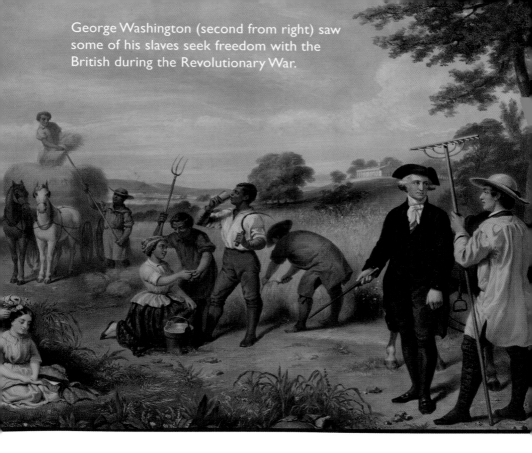

George Washington (second from right) saw some of his slaves seek freedom with the British during the Revolutionary War.

very much dissatisfied at being discarded." Congress agreed that "the free negroes who have served faithfully in the army at Cambridge, may be re-inlisted … but no others."

Despite his mixed feelings about having blacks under his command, Washington saw their usefulness and began to doubt the morality of slavery. At the Battle of Long Island in late August 1776, he and his men had to make a hasty retreat after a British victory. Many of the ships used to ferry the men to Manhattan came from Massachusetts fishing communities. Blacks often worked on ships in the American Colonies, and the fleet that carried Washington's men to safety included about 150 black sailors.

The same fighting fishermen also helped Washington's army cross the Delaware River in late December. The crossing was part of a successful plan to surprise Hessian forces based in Trenton, New Jersey. The early morning crossing wasn't easy, as the boats sailed around chunks of ice during a harsh snowstorm. But the patriots safely crossed the river and surprised the enemy forces. The Battle of Trenton was Washington's first major victory of the war.

Another important victory came a week later at Princeton. Among those present was Primus Hall, a black soldier in the Continental army. The son of free blacks from Boston, Hall's one-year term of military service ended after Trenton. But before he went home, Hall and others listened as Washington pleaded with them to re-enlist. Hall heeded Washington's call, and as a result, he witnessed the general's military savvy in action.

Outside Princeton, Washington instructed his men to build huge fires. When the British saw the fiery orange glow, they thought the Americans had set up their camp for the night. Instead, Washington moved his men to a position where they could launch a surprise attack. On the morning of January 3, 1777, as American cannons roared, Washington rode among his men encouraging them to fight. During the action Primus Hall chased after two fleeing Redcoats before finally capturing them both and taking them prisoner.

Emanuel Leutze's original 1850 version of *Washington Crossing the Delaware* was destroyed during World War II. However, Leutze had completed a second version (seen here) in 1851.

Did You *Know?*

Emanuel Leutze's famous painting *Washington Crossing the Delaware* shows a black man (third from left) rowing the general's boat. Some historians think this is Prince Whipple. He had come to America from Africa in 1760 and was the slave of William Whipple, one of Washington's aides.

CHAPTER Three

A Growing Role for Blacks

Despite the American success at Trenton, the war was approaching the two-year mark, and no end was in sight. The Continental army needed soldiers, so it sought more blacks to help with the war effort. It offered money, called a bounty, to men who joined. In some cases masters signed up their slaves so they could claim the bounty. Some slaves received written documents guaranteeing their freedom in return for serving in place of their masters. Others were given their freedom even before they ever saw battle.

Although the black population in the New England states was relatively small, they recruited the greatest number of black soldiers for the Continental army. By the summer of 1778, there were about 750 blacks in the Continental army. During the entire war about 6,600 blacks and American Indians served in the army, and more worked as sailors or fought in the militias.

Five Ways Blacks Could Serve
During the Revolutionary War

Slaves could escape to fight for the British.

Slaves could serve as substitutes for white masters.

Escaped slaves could lie about their status and
join a militia group or the American forces.

Free blacks could enlist in order to receive a bounty.

Slaves could be bought by state governments
and freed upon completion of service.

Some of these northern blacks served under George Washington at Valley Forge, Pennsylvania, during the winter of 1777–1778. For weeks men froze in tattered clothes, went barefoot because of a lack of shoes, and often died from disease. Men cried out in hunger, desperate for food after having none for days. Others scratched their bodies endlessly from a skin disease that was passed around the camp.

Nero Hawley of North Stratford, Connecticut, was among those suffering through the horrible conditions at Valley Forge that winter. As a slave, Hawley had enlisted in the Continental army during the spring of 1777. He received a bounty and the promise of his future freedom. Several other black men from his town also joined the army. They fought in just one small skirmish against the British before winter began.

After surviving the brutal winter at Valley Forge, Hawley served as an army scout for several years. He was wounded during a battle in 1779 and left the army in 1781. He was granted his freedom the following year.

Baron Friedrich Wilhelm von Steuben was popular among the ragged troops at Valley Forge, even though he worked them extremely hard.

Rhode Island's Contribution

Although it was the smallest of the colonies, Rhode Island had some plantations with fairly large slave populations. As a result, it enlisted a large number of black soldiers—more than 700 in the course of the war. Rhode Island was also the only colony to field an entire regiment of blacks. The decision to form the 1st Rhode Island Regiment came in early 1778. The British had just captured Newport, the state's major seaport, and Rhode Island feared losing its sea trade. General James Varnum of Rhode Island suggested the idea of creating a black regiment, and Washington gave his approval. In the state's call for black soldiers, it promised that as soon as a slave enlisted he would "be immediately discharged from the service of his master or mistress, and be absolutely FREE."

Using His Head

Even before the 1st Rhode Island Regiment was formed, one of its future members played a role in the Revolutionary War. When Colonel William Barton planned a daring midnight raid on the British, he chose his former servant Jack Sisson to help. Sisson was one of 40 men who snuck through British lines and into the house of General Richard Prescott on July 10, 1777. Sisson piloted one of the boats used during the raid. It is also believed that he used his head to knock down a door in Prescott's house! Sisson and the others managed to escape with Prescott as a prisoner. Prescott was later exchanged for U.S. General Charles Lee, who had been captured by the British in December 1776.

By the summer of 1778, the 1st Rhode Island Regiment had about 130 black soldiers under the command of General John Sullivan. More signed up as the war progressed. That August the regiment joined other patriots in battling the British in Newport. The members of the 1st Rhode Island Regiment proved their worth when the fighting began in Newport on August 29. With cannons booming across the battlefield, the British soldiers charged the Americans. Hessians fighting for the British rushed toward the 1st Rhode Island Regiment. The black Rhode Islanders stood their ground and unleashed heavy fire that drove back the Hessians. The Hessians soon came back with more troops, but the blazing guns of the black Americans forced the Hessians to retreat. The Hessians tried to advance one more time, and once again, the 1st Rhode Island Regiment held them off.

The next year, as the main battles of the war moved to the South, soldiers in the 1st Rhode Island Regiment went along. They also fought in New York in 1781. During the Battle of Points Bridge, the Rhode Islanders were taken by surprise. Several of the black soldiers died while bravely trying to protect their commanding officer, Colonel Christopher Greene.

Did You Know?

After the fierce fighting at Newport, a Hessian officer resigned his post. He felt that if his men had to face the 1st Rhode Island Regiment again, he'd be leading them to slaughter, and he didn't want to be responsible for that.

The 1st Rhode Island Regiment courageously pushed back the Hessians during the Battle of Rhode Island in Newport.

According to reports, Greene's faithful black troops surrounded him in an attempt to protect him from the enemy's bayonets. Despite their efforts, Colonel Greene and those attempting to save him were all killed.

Fighting a Traitor

In 1779 American General Benedict Arnold turned his back on the patriot cause. Two years later, in September 1781, Arnold and 800 British troops sailed up the Thames River in Connecticut and set fire to the towns of New London and Groton. The patriots who could escape headed to nearby Fort Griswold, but the Redcoats followed them in hot pursuit. At Fort Griswold, the British attacked Colonel William Ledyard and about 150 Americans who were defending the fort. Although they were heavily outnumbered, the Americans put up a courageous fight.

Among the Americans fighting that day were Jordan Freeman and Lambert Latham, two black men from Connecticut. Freeman had been Colonel Ledyard's slave. After being granted his freedom, Freeman decided to fight alongside his former master.

Lambert Latham was a slave who was working with his master, Captain William Latham, in a nearby field when the fighting erupted. He too followed his master into the battle. Despite receiving a severe bullet wound to his hand, Lambert Latham continued to load and fire a musket at the enemy.

Inside Fort Griswold, Freeman, Latham, and others looked on as British soldiers clambered over the fort's walls. Freeman and another man grabbed a spear and killed British officer William Montgomery as soon as he scaled the wall. That only enraged the Redcoats, who quickly began a massacre once inside the fort.

When a British officer asked, "Who commands this fort?" Ledyard handed over his sword and replied, "I did sir, but you do now." Despite Ledyard's peaceful surrender, the British officer grabbed the colonel's sword and stabbed him with it.

After Ledyard was killed, it was Lambert Latham who rammed his bayonet through the British officer who had killed the colonel. By the end of the fighting, Lambert Latham, Jordan Freeman, their masters, and dozens of others were dead. By one account, Lambert Latham's dead body suffered 33 stab wounds from British bayonets.

Blacks in the South

As the war dragged on, many southerners still opposed recruiting blacks, whether they were slaves or free. Virginia did allow 150 free blacks and 25 slaves to fight,

A 135-foot (41-meter) monument stands where the Battle of Fort Griswold took place in Groton, Connecticut, on September 6, 1781. It is dedicated to the American troops who were massacred by the British during the battle.

although Governor Thomas Nelson noted that it seemed unfair. In a letter to George Washington, he expressed his opinion that "after they have risk'd their lives [and] … contributed to save America, [they] will not be entitled to the privileges of Freemen."

Maryland—the only southern state that let slaves serve in the militia—recruited blacks, both free and slave. Some masters in South Carolina sold their slaves to the Continental army. Southern slaves usually worked as laborers in the army rather than as gun-toting soldiers.

However, some southern blacks did see action on the battlefield or on the water. Maryland, Virginia, and South Carolina relied on black pilots to captain ships on rivers or close to shore. These pilots and black crewmen included free blacks, slaves serving in place of their masters, and runaway slaves.

One of the most famous pilots was Caesar Tarrant, a slave from Hampton, Virginia. He sailed small, armed boats for most of the war. On one voyage while piloting the *Patriot*, he purposely plowed his boat into a larger, better-armed British vessel. Another time he and his crew captured an enemy vessel that was carrying supplies to Boston. After the war the state of Virginia bought Tarrant from his master and set him free.

On land most blacks served as privates, often working at jobs away from the battlefield, such as cooks or waiters for officers. (This was true for northern blacks as well.) But those who fought showed battlefield heroics time and again. A few earned distinction like Austin Dabney, who served in the Georgia militia in place of his master. When a bullet pierced Dabney's leg during the Battle of Kettle Creek in 1779, a white soldier took Dabney to his house to recover. After the war, Dabney received 112 acres (45 hectares) of land and his freedom as a reward for his heroic service during several battles.

Seeking More Blacks

Most southern lawmakers and masters did not want to use slaves in the militia even as the need for soldiers increased.

But John Laurens of South Carolina had a different view. Although his family owned slaves, Laurens strongly believed that slavery was wrong.

At the time Laurens' father, Henry, was the president of the Continental Congress. In 1778 John suggested to his father that South Carolina use slaves as soldiers, promising them their freedom in return. Because the southern white men were reluctant to fight for the patriot cause, blacks would provide much-needed troops.

John Laurens

"A well chosen body of 5,000 black men, properly officer'd to act as light Troops … might give us decisive Success in the next Campaign."

—John Laurens, in a letter to his father, February 2, 1778

At first the elder Laurens resisted his son's idea. But as the British sent troops to seize Charleston, the capital of South Carolina, the need for more troops increased. Henry Laurens began to support the idea, and Congress called on both Georgia and South Carolina to recruit 5,000 slaves for the militia. The recruits would receive their freedom and $50 when the war ended—if they survived. Slave owners would receive money in exchange for their slaves.

But state lawmakers disliked the idea of recruiting slaves, and both states quickly rejected the suggestion. Even as fighting in the South intensified, they would not consider arming slaves and training them as soldiers.

Other Roles for Blacks

Although southern states were not eager to arm slaves, they did value their work in other aspects of the war effort. With many white men off to battle, the states needed workers to mine, make iron, and work as carpenters and blacksmiths. Blacks also played important roles as spies and messengers.

A slave named Saul Matthews served as a guide and spy for Colonel Josiah Parker. Matthews entered British-held land and then reported back to Parker with valuable military secrets. Nearly 10 years after the war, Matthews formally petitioned for his freedom. For the "very essential services" he contributed during the war, he was granted "full liberty and freedom … as if he had been born free."

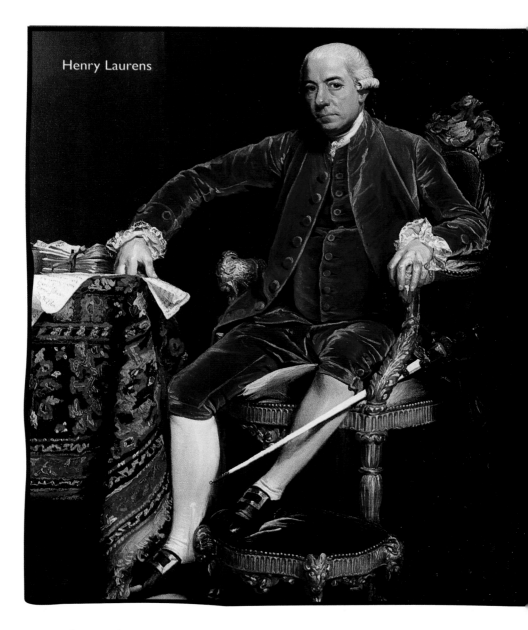

Henry Laurens

Until recently most history books have ignored or discounted the role of black soldiers, sailors, and laborers in the Revolutionary War. However, when given a chance, the black patriots did all they could in the fight for America's independence.

CHAPTER *Four*

Fighting for the British

From the start of the war, the British faced the same problem the Americans did: They needed more soldiers. Britain had the added problem of needing weeks to send new troops from Europe to North America. One solution was to rely on white loyalists. Another was to do what Lord Dunmore had done in 1775: offer the slaves of patriots their freedom if they left their masters and fought for the British. For the slaves, however, running away to join the British was especially dangerous. If their masters caught them, they faced punishment and perhaps even death.

Lord Dunmore had been the first British official to see the value of arming black soldiers for the king's cause. In the South blacks overwhelmingly escaped to the British.

Yet on the battlefield, Dunmore's Ethiopian Regiment had met with only mixed success.

The Ethiopian Regiment first saw action just after Dunmore issued his late-1775 proclamation. On November 14 a small number of Dunmore's black soldiers battled a patriot militia group at Kemp's Landing, near present-day Virginia Beach. Firing from behind thick bushes, the Americans, led by Colonel Joseph Hutchings, opened fire on Dunmore's forces. Dunmore ordered some of his men, including the Ethiopian Regiment, to circle around the American militiamen. Blacks and whites were now fighting side by side against the Americans.

By the Numbers

450,000   Estimated slave population at the start of the Revolutionalry War; about 20 percent of the total population

100,000   Estimated number of slaves who escaped, died, or were killed during the Revolutionary War; about 22 percent of the slave population

50,000   Estimated number of slaves who served with the British during the Revolutionary War

6,600   Estimated number of slaves who fought for the Americans during the Revolutionary War

Before he could take cover in the swampy waters nearby, Colonel Hutchings noticed a familiar face coming toward him. It was one of his former slaves, who was now fighting for the British. Hutchings fired his gun and missed. The former slave swung his sword at Hutchings, and several black soldiers hauled him off as a prisoner.

The Ethiopian Regiment tasted defeat the following month. During a skirmish outside Norfolk, Virginia, a larger patriot force attacked the British and

A black militiaman during the Revolutionary War

drove off the Ethiopian Regiment, killing or wounding several men in the process. During the battle a black patriot named William Flora fired on the Ethiopian Regiment. Although many black Americans found themselves on opposite sides during the long war, they still shared a common goal— winning their freedom through military service.

In most cases, the British and the patriots offered slaves their freedom not because they believed blacks were equal or deserved certain rights, but rather they simply wanted to win the war. And they needed all the manpower they could get. Using blacks was one way to do it.

From the slaves' perspective, most were only concerned about winning their freedom. They didn't care why it was being offered, even though they'd be risking their lives if they fought.

Blacks in Action

Although the Ethiopian Regiment struggled with disease and battlefield losses, many saw action later in the war. In 1776 Lord Dunmore sent 300 black soldiers north to New York. There they joined General William Howe's army for its 1777 campaign to capture Philadelphia, the U.S. capital at the time. During the summer Howe moved about 15,000 troops from New York to Maryland and then to Pennsylvania. Dunmore also sent about 500 slaves to fight the patriots in exchange for their freedom.

On September 11, Howe's army defeated George Washington and his men at Brandywine, outside Philadelphia. By the end of the month, the British had seized the American capital.

Freedom at Any Cost

Patriot slave owners from Pennsylvania thought they treated their slaves pretty well, so they didn't think their slaves would run away and join the British in return for their freedom. They were wrong. While the British controlled Philadelphia, hundreds of slaves fled to fight for the Crown. A minister in Philadelphia wrote that the slaves of patriot owners "secretly wished that the British army might win," thinking the victory would bring all slaves their freedom.

Many more blacks served as soldiers for the British than for the Americans. In both the North and South, many blacks also worked as guides, helping the British move quickly through unfamiliar areas. Other blacks served as spies. These spies and guides were sometimes called the Black Pioneers. They also performed strenuous tasks, such as building temporary forts and moving supplies.

One slave who helped guide the British was Quamino Dolly. In November 1778, when the

British began a new strategy of fighting the Americans mostly in the South, Georgia was their first target. When British troops came ashore in Savannah on December 29, Dolly greeted them. He told Colonel Archibald Campbell that he knew a secret path through the local swamps. He offered to guide Campbell and his men in exchange for his freedom. Campbell agreed, and the British followed Dolly as he trekked through the swampland. The American soldiers guarding the forests around the swamps didn't hear the British coming.

Washington's troops tried desperately to hold off a British assault at the Battle of Brandywine. But after losing nearly 1,300 men, they were forced to retreat.

As the British forces attacked from the front and rear, many patriots ran into the swamp, only to drown or be attacked by alligators. Campbell's men took Savannah with almost no casualties. And in the weeks that followed, Campbell recruited more local slaves to help him. But if the slaves of loyalists fled their masters in order to enlist, he tried to capture them and return them.

Boston King also helped the British. King ran away from his master at age 18, after receiving many severe beatings. He fled to Charleston, South Carolina, where he met up with a small group of Redcoats, who had captured the city in May 1780. A much larger American force was in the area, but the British had around 1,200 men about 30 miles (48 kilometers) away.

King offered to walk the 30 miles to seek reinforcements for the commander. King knew the dangers he faced because the Americans controlled most of the countryside. Despite the potential danger, King successfully completed his mission to send word for reinforcements.

"I expected every moment to fall in with the enemy, whom I well knew would show me no mercy."

—Boston King, recalling his mission for the British

A New Policy

As the southern campaign unfolded, large numbers of blacks escaped their patriot masters and joined the British. Then in June 1779, General Henry Clinton issued the Philipsburg Proclamation. As Lord Dunmore had done, Clinton promised freedom to blacks who joined the British. But this time the freedom seekers were not mainly expected to fight. An escaped slave only had to work at "any occupation which he shall think proper." Clinton also told the slaves that if they stayed with their masters and then were captured, the British would sell them to new masters. Only the ones who escaped had the chance to taste freedom.

General Henry Clinton

The proclamation led many more blacks to leave their masters than Clinton had anticipated. Sources vary, but by one estimate as many 100,000 slaves across the South ran away to join the British. Some came alone or in pairs. Other times entire families fled, or a large group of slaves ran away from the same plantation.

The British knew that southern loyalists did not want blacks to have guns, even if they were fighting a common enemy. Still, when the situation demanded it, blacks fired rifles and manned cannons. After losing Savannah to the British in 1778, the Americans attempted a counterattack in 1779. About 250 blacks were among those helping to successfully defend the city.

As in the Continental army, blacks serving the British also piloted small boats along the coast and up rivers. They also worked as crew members on small British ships that attacked coastal towns. One Virginia official was distressed that "our own Negroes who have run off" were now raiding his county.

Colonel Tye

Of the blacks who battled the patriots, one of the most famous was a slave named Tye (or Titus). He was called "colonel" out of respect, although he didn't actually hold that rank.

Tye fled his New Jersey master soon after Lord Dunmore issued his 1775 proclamation. He went to Virginia to join the Ethiopian Regiment and then returned north. He led the Black Brigade, a band of loyalist guerrillas who struck fear into the patriots in New Jersey.

Colonel Tye and his men roamed the countryside looking for supplies to send to loyalists in New York. On one of their first

Did You Know?

Female slaves who joined the British also helped with the war effort. Some prepared cartridges for British guns. Others helped treat wounded soldiers in military hospitals.

raids in 1779, they stole cattle and horses from patriot farms. They also spiked guns or cannons by placing metal rods in them, which made the weapons useless. Tye and his men sometimes killed or captured patriot militia leaders and took them to British officials in New York. In March 1780 Tye burned the home of John Russell, a patriot who raided loyalist homes.

Tye's last raid came in September 1780 when his men surrounded the home of Josiah Huddy, a patriot militia commander. Huddy had bragged of hanging a local loyalist, and Tye wanted revenge. For a while Huddy held off Tye's guerrillas by running from room to room shooting at them. But after a couple hours of gunfire, Tye's men set fire to the house. Tye was injured during the shooting, and he later died from his wounds.

By the end of 1781, the British were losing the war in the South. Hoping to prevent defeat, Lord Dunmore once more proposed arming blacks and hoped to raise an army of 10,000 black soldiers. As with past plans, slaves who enlisted would win their freedom. But Dunmore's new plan went nowhere because it wasn't long before British leaders in London abandoned the war effort.

The End of the War and After

Lord Dunmore's new plan to arm escaped slaves showed how badly the war was going for the British. Their campaign in the South started well, but by 1781 the Americans were gaining strength.

With more than 800 British soldiers wounded, killed, or captured, the Battle of Cowpens was a turning point in the southern campaign of the war.

In January the patriots won a major victory at the Battle of Cowpens, in South Carolina. Blacks took part in that battle on the patriot side. They and the other Americans were led by General Daniel Morgan, who knew British troops were approaching. Rather than retreat, Morgan decided to stay and fight.

Over the din of shouts and screams, the British swarmed ahead firing their guns. The patriots accurately returned fire, then charged with their bayonets. At the rear Colonel William Washington, a cousin of George Washington, led his cavalry troops into the battle. During the assault, a young slave named William Bell spotted a British officer about to kill Colonel Washington. Bell shot and killed the enemy before he could attack.

The Battle of Yorktown

During 1781 the main fighting in the South moved up through the Carolinas and into Virginia. By September about 7,000 British troops had reached Yorktown, Virginia, but they were soon trapped there by an onslaught of patriots. General George Washington and French troops marched into Yorktown from the north. French ships delivered 3,000 more men and prevented British ships from getting close enough to shore to attack the patriots. Boosting the Continental army's strength were American troops who were already in Virginia under the command of a young French general known as the Marquis de Lafayette.

Among Lafayette's forces was James Armistead, a slave who had received permission from his master to volunteer for the patriot cause. As the American troops moved closer to Yorktown, Armistead offered to spy on the British.

James Armistead

Lafayette sent him to the camp of General Benedict Arnold, who had recently switched his loyalty to the British. Posing as a runaway slave, Armistead offered his services to the British in return for his freedom. He led troops through the countryside and won the trust of Lord Cornwallis, who was in command of the British forces in the southern states. When the British openly discussed their plans for future raids on patriot targets, Armistead wrote down what they said. He then relayed it to other American spies, who took the information to Lafayette's camp. With Armistead's help, patriot soldiers

After the war James Armistead won his freedom, thanks mostly to the support he received from the Marquis de Lafayette. In return, Armistead began using Lafayette as his last name.

even snuck into the British camp and nearly captured Benedict Arnold as a prisoner.

The British were completely unaware that Armistead was spying for the patriots. In fact, Cornwallis asked Armistead to go to the American camp and spy for him! Armistead played the role of double agent well. He continued to gather information about the location of British troops for Lafayette without the British learning his true loyalties. Armistead proved an invaluable asset to the American victory in the Battle of Yorktown.

At Yorktown, the American and French strategy was simple: The French controlled the waters nearby, so the British could not escape by boat. They also outnumbered the British. On October 9 American and French cannons began firing on the British almost nonstop for several days. After nearly a week, the enemy was weakened, so the patriots marched forward.

At Yorktown the 1st Rhode Island Regiment demonstrated both bravery and military might. They joined black troops from Connecticut and Massachusetts on the night of October 14 and attacked two centrally located forts called redoubts. The black soldiers silently crept up on the redoubts and prepared to fight with their bayonets.

Soon gunfire sprayed out from the redoubts, cutting down some of the black patriots. With the silence broken, the Rhode Islanders let out a war cry and returned fire. Soon cannon fire lit up the night sky. Despite the chaos, the black soldiers focused on their goal and captured the redoubts. From there the Americans were able to aim their cannons directly at the British positions. Knowing he was defeated, Cornwallis soon surrendered.

According to Baron Ludwig von Closen, a German officer serving in the French army, black soldiers made up about 25 percent of the Continental army at Yorktown. They played a key role in the battle as they had throughout the war. And while some fighting continued after Yorktown, the American victory there was crucial. When British leaders heard of Cornwallis' defeat, they decided to end the conflict. Yorktown was the last major battle of the Revolutionary War, and it guaranteed American independence.

Did You Know?

When Cornwallis went to the headquarters of Lafayette to work out the terms of surrender, he was greeted by a familiar face in a patriot uniform—his spy, James Armistead.

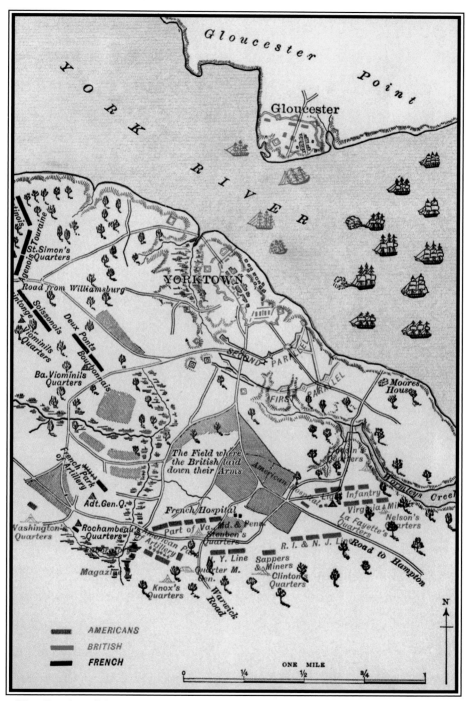

The Battle of Yorktown was a game-changing victory for the patriots.

Freedom—for Some

During and soon after the war, several northern states took steps to end slavery. Vermont outlawed bondage in 1777. When Massachusetts approved a new state constitution in 1780, it stated, "All men are born free and equal."

Pennsylvania passed a law in 1780 that gradually abolished slavery in the state. Between 1784 and 1804, Rhode Island, Connecticut, New York, and New Jersey did the same. Together these states created the free North that would later fight to abolish slavery during the Civil War.

While the movement to end slavery grew slowly, the Revolutionary War gave it boost. Many white Americans realized that it was hypocritical to talk about their own freedom while enslaving others.

When the war ended, slaves who had fought for the patriots expected their freedom, and most of them received it. In a few cases, though, masters broke their promises to free slaves who fought in their place or had received permission to volunteer. When a Connecticut slave named Jack Arabas returned home after serving for three years, his master denied that he was free. Arabas went to court and eventually won the freedom he had been promised.

Some slaves found that their efforts during the war led to their freedom even if it had not been promised to them. In 1781 a Virginia slave named Latchom was part of the local militia fighting off a British assault. His commander, General John Cropper, got stuck in a marsh, where he was an easy target for approaching British soldiers. Before a British soldier

Young Sailor to Wealthy Sailmaker

James Forten volunteered for the war effort in 1781. While some blacks fought for their freedom, Forten was already free. A sense of patriotism inspired him to sign on to a privateer, but a British naval ship captured his boat.

Rather than sending Forten to the West Indies to be sold back into slavery, the ship's captain, John Bazely, offered to send Forten to England to get an education. Forten declined the offer out of loyalty to his country. As a result Forten was sent to the *Jersey*, a notoriously wretched prison ship. He spent seven months there before being released in a prisoner exchange in 1782.

After his release Forten briefly returned home and then became a sailor on a merchant ship. By 1798 he had his own sail-making business. Forten became one of the wealthiest citizens in Philadelphia, and he used his money to support the abolition of slavery. In 2014 he became the first black hero of the American Revolution honored by the city of Philadelphia.

James Forten

could stab Cropper with his bayonet, Latchom shot and killed the enemy. When the war ended, the grateful Cropper bought Latchom from his master and freed him.

Blacks and the British

With the war over, British officials wanted to honor the promise they had made to the black loyalists—blacks who had run away and fought for them. The Americans argued against this practice because some patriots, particularly in the South, wanted their slaves back. But as the British left the United States, thousands of blacks went with them.

Although the British offered many African-Americans the chance to earn their freedom, some who came into British hands remained enslaved. British officers gave captured patriot slaves to loyalists who had lost their own. Some officers kept slaves for themselves and made them into servants. Other slaves left America with their loyalist owners. Many of them settled in Florida, while others went to British colonies in the Caribbean or north to Canada. Some headed for Great Britain.

By the time the British left New York in 1783, they had signed a peace treaty with the Americans. Although the treaty said the British could not take any blacks with them, many did. General Guy Carleton, the British commander in New York, claimed that most of the blacks leaving with the British were free. In a letter to George Washington written in May 1783, Carleton stated: "The negroes in question … I found free when I arrived at New York, I had therefore no right … to prevent their going to any part of the World they thought proper." He said American slave owners who lost their slaves could seek payment later. As a result Carleton compiled the *Book of Negroes*, which recorded the names of 3,000 blacks who left New York.

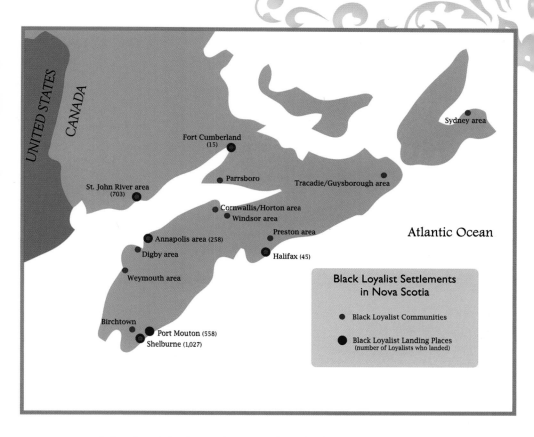

Black Loyalist Settlements in Nova Scotia

- United States
- Canada
- Sydney area
- Fort Cumberland (15)
- Parrsboro
- Tracadie/Guysborough area
- St. John River area (703)
- Cornwallis/Horton area
- Windsor area
- Preston area
- Atlantic Ocean
- Annapolis area (258)
- Digby area
- Halifax (45)
- Weymouth area
- Birchtown
- Port Mouton (558)
- Shelburne (1,027)

Black Loyalist Communities

Black Loyalist Landing Places
(number of Loyalists who landed)

Most of the free blacks and newly freed black loyalists who left New York went to Nova Scotia, Canada. The British promised them land there, but they often received little or none. Still, many tried to make a living in their new home. Colonel Stephen Blucke of the Black Brigade helped start Birchtown, in southwestern Nova Scotia. It was one of the first all-black towns in North America and the largest of its kind at the time. Many indentured servants and newly freed blacks also settled in Shelburne, Nova Scotia.

In 1792 more than 1,100 free blacks sailed from Nova Scotia in Canada to establish Freetown, Sierra Leone, West Africa.

Boston King, who had made a heroic ride seeking reinforcements for the British, also settled in Nova Scotia for a while. In all, about 3,500 free blacks moved there immediately following the Revolutionary War.

Over time though, many blacks became frustrated by discrimination and the harsh climate of Nova Scotia. The British government offered them the opportunity to establish a new settlement called Freetown in Sierra Leone, West Africa. Henry Washington, one of George Washington's former slaves, and Boston King were among about 1,100 free blacks who moved from Nova Scotia to Sierra Leone.

Independence and Freedom

The black soldiers of the Revolutionary War knew that the war was about the 13 American Colonies winning their independence from Great Britain. But for most of the black soldiers, the war was also about winning their own personal freedom. Fighting for both sides, several thousand did achieve that goal, but many more remained enslaved. Although the Revolutionary War did eventually result in the emancipation of the northern states, many Americans—both black and white—still hoped to abolish slavery all across America. But it would take another long and even bloodier conflict—the Civil War— to give all black Americans the liberty they sought and deserved.

1754–1763: Blacks help white colonists and British soldiers fight the French and Indian War.

1765: Americans protest the Stamp Act.

March 5, 1770: Crispus Attucks leads the attack on British soldiers during the Boston Massacre.

1773: Slaves of Massachusetts petition for their freedom.

April 19, 1775: Prince Estabrook takes part in the first battle of the Revolutionary War at Lexington, Massachusetts; both free and enslaved blacks take part in the fighting throughout the day.

November 7, 1775: Lord Dunmore, the royal governor of Virginia, offers slaves their freedom if they will fight for the British; the Continental Congress votes to keep blacks out of the Continental army.

December 1775: George Washington allows the recruiting of free blacks in the Continental army.

September 1776: Black sailors help transport defeated American troops to safety.

December 26, 1776: Black sailors help George Washington and his men cross the Delaware River before the Battle of Trenton.

1777: Jack Sisson takes part in the capture of British General Richard Prescott.

1778: Rhode Island forms an all-black regiment.

June 30, 1779: General Henry Clinton issues the Philipsburg Proclamation, offering slaves their freedom if they work for the British.

1780: "Colonel" Tye leads raids against patriots.

1781: James Armistead serves as a double-agent spy and gathers information on British forces.

January 17, 1781: The Americans win a significant victory at the Battle of Cowpens, which proves to be a turning point in the southern campaign of the war.

September 29, 1781: The Siege of Yorktown begins and lasts for three weeks as American and French troops pound the British in what would be the last major battle of the war.

October 19, 1781: British General Cornwallis formally surrenders in Yorktown.

April 11, 1783: The Revolutionary War officially ends.

1783: The British leave New York with 3,000 blacks; most are now free and head to Canada.

1792: Unhappy with the conditions in Nova Scotia, Canada, approximately 1,100 free blacks sail to Sierra Leone, West Africa, to settle Freetown.

Glossary

artillery—large guns, such as cannons, that require several soldiers to load, aim, and fire

fife—a small musical instrument similar to a flute

guerrilla—a member of a small group of fighters who carry out surprise attacks against enemy forces

Hessian—a German soldier hired by the British

indentured servant—a person who works for someone else for a certain period of time in return for payment of travel and living costs

integrate—to bring people of different races together in schools and other public places

loyalist—a colonist loyal to Great Britain during the Revolutionary War

manslaughter—killing another person without intending to do so

military governor—a military officer in command of an area that has been taken over or conquered by another country

militia—a group of volunteer citizens organized to fight but who are not professional soldiers

Minutemen—colonists who were ready and willing to fight at a moment's notice during the Revolutionary War

Parliament—the national legislature of Great Britain

patriot—a person who sided with the American Colonies during the Revolutionary War

petition—a collection of signatures showing support for an issue

privateer—a private ship that is authorized to attack enemy ships during wartime

recruit—to seek out someone for a job or organization

Redcoats—the nickname given to British soldiers during the Revolutionary War because of the color of their uniforms

redoubt—a small building or area that protects soldiers under attack

reinforcements—extra troops sent into battle

Further Reading

Blair, Margaret Whitman. *Liberty or Death: The Surprising Story of Runaway Slaves Who Sided with the British During the American Revolution.* Washington, D.C.: National Geographic, 2010.

Micklos, John. *American Indians and African Americans of the American Revolution—Through Primary Sources.* Berkeley Heights, N.J.: Enslow Publishers, Inc., 2013.

Raatma, Lucia. *African-American Soldiers in the Revolutionary War.* Minneapolis, Minn.: Compass Point Books, 2009.

Rockwell, Anne F. *The Other Double Agent: The True Story of James Armistead Lafayette, the Revolutionary Spy No One Has Ever Heard of (Because He Didn't Get Caught).* Minneapolis: Carolrhoda Books, 2015.

Shea, Therese. *The Boston Massacre.* New York: Gareth Stevens Publishing, 2014.

Internet Sites

Use Facthound to find Internet sites related to this book. All of the sites on FactHound have been researched by our staff.

Here's all you do:

Visit *www.facthound.com*

Type in this code: 9780756549756

Critical Thinking Using the Common Core

1. Why were some commanders, including George Washington, reluctant to allow slaves to fight in the Revolutionary War? (Key Ideas and Details)

2. Look at the map on page 51. How does it help to explain how the French and American forces defeated the British at the Battle of Yorktown? (Integration of Knowledge and Ideas)

3. The Revolutionary War was fought so the United States could win its independence from Great Britain. But for black slaves, it was also about gaining their personal freedom. Using logical reasoning and relevant evidence from the text, explain how events during and right after the Revolutionary War set the stage for the Civil War in the 1860s. (Text Types and Purposes)

Source Notes

Page 13, sidebar, line 5: Gary B. Nash. *Race and Revolution*. Madison, Wis.: Madison House, 1990, p. 173.

Page 15, col. 1, line 13: Henry Steele Commager and Richard B. Morris, eds. *The Spirit of 'Seventy-Six: The Story of the American Revolution as Told by Participants.* New York: Harper & Row, 1967, p. 81.

Page 15, col. 2, line 1: Thomas Fleming. *Liberty!: The American Revolution.* New York: Viking, 1997, p. 113.

Page 17, col. 2, line 10: Sidney Kaplan and Emma Nogrady Kaplan. *The Black Presence in the Era of the American Revolution.* Amherst, Mass.: University of Massachusetts Press, 1989, pp. 22–23.

Page 19, sidebar, line 1: "Africans in America: Revolution." 25 Nov. 2014. http://www.pbs.org/wgbh/aia/part2/2h42b.html

Page 20, col. 2, line 25: Gail Buckley. *American Patriots: The Story of Blacks in the Military from the Revolution to Desert Storm.* New York: Random House, 2001, p. 16.

Page 21, col. 1, line 3: *Journals of the Continental Congress, 1774–1789*, Vol. IV, 1776, Washington, D.C.: Government Printing Office, p. 60.

Page 27, col. 2, line 11: Alan Gilbert. *Black Patriots and Loyalists: Fighting for Emancipation in the War for Independence.* Chicago: The University of Chicago Press, 2012, p. 99.

Page 31, col. 1, line 5: Frank E. Grizzard Jr. and David R. Hoth, eds. *The Papers of George Washington, Revolutionary War Series, vol. 12, 26 October 1777–25 December 1777.* Charlottesville: University Press of Virginia, 2002, pp. 341–343.

Page 33, callout quote: William Gilmore Simms. *The Army Correspondence of Colonel John Laurens in the Years 1777–8.* New York: Bradford Club, 1867, p. 117.

Page 34, col. 2, line 19: *The Black Presence in the Era of the American Revolution,* p. 59.

Page 40, col. 1, line 13: Gary B. Nash. *The Forgotten Fifth: African Americans in the Age of Revolution.* Cambridge, Mass.: Harvard University Press, 2006, p. 30.

Page 42, callout quote: *Black Patriots and Loyalists: Fighting for Emancipation in the War for Independence,* p. 118.

Page 43, col. 1, line 3: Gary B. Nash. *The Unknown American Revolution: The Unruly Birth of Democracy and the Struggle to Create America.* New York: Viking, 2005, p. 331.

Page 44, col. 1, line 8: *Collections of the Virginia Historical Society*, Volume 11, by Virginia Historical Society, 1891, p. 294.

Page 52, col. 1, line 7: The Constitution of Massachusetts, 1780. National Humanities Institute. 6 Nov. 2014. http://www.nhinet.org/ccs/docs/ma-1780.htm

Page 54, col. 2, line 15: *Black Patriots and Loyalists: Fighting for Emancipation in the War for Independence,* p. 190.

Select Bibliography

Boatner, Mark M. III. *Encyclopedia of the American Revolution.* Mechanicsburg, Pa.: Stackpole Books, 1994.

Buckley, Gail. *American Patriots: The Story of Blacks in the Military from the Revolution to Desert Storm.* New York: Random House, 2001.

Commager, Henry Steele, and Richard B. Morris, eds. *The Spirit of 'Seventy-Six: The Story of the American Revolution as Told by Participants.* New York: Harper & Row, 1967.

Fleming, Thomas J. *Liberty!: The American Revolution.* New York: Viking, 1997.

Gilbert, Alan. *Black Patriots and Loyalists: Fighting for Emancipation in the War for Independence.* Chicago: The University of Chicago Press, 2012.

Horton, James Oliver, and Lois E. Horton. *Slavery and the Making of America.* New York: Oxford University Press, 2005.

Nash, Gary B. *The Forgotten Fifth: African Americans in the Age of Revolution.* Cambridge, Mass.: Harvard University Press, 2006.

Nash, Gary B. *The Unknown American Revolution: The Unruly Birth of Democracy and the Struggle to Create America.* New York: Viking, 2005.

Quarles, Benjamin. *The Negro in the American Revolution.* New York: W. W. Norton & Company, 1973.

Schama, Simon. *Rough Crossings: Britain, the Slaves, and the American Revolution.* New York: Ecco, 2006.

Schneider, Dorothy, and Carl J. Schneider. *Slavery in America: From Colonial Times to the Civil War.* New York: Facts on File, 2000.

Sheeler, J. Reuben. "The Negro on the Virginia Frontier." *The Journal of Negro History*, Vol. 43, No. 4, Oct. 1958, pp. 279–297.

Ward, Harry M. *For Virginia and for Independence: Twenty-Eight Revolutionary War Soldiers from the Old Dominion.* Jefferson, N.C.: McFarland & Co., 2011.

Index

About the Author

Michael Burgan has written more than 250 books for children and teens, mostly on U.S. history. He specializes in the Colonial era and the period just before and after the American Revolution. Michael lives in Santa Fe, New Mexico.

MAR 1 0 2016